Ears That Hear

By Chance Little
Illustrated by Keishart

Library For All Ltd.

I don't remember when
my ear trouble started.
I've had it since I was little.

I remember having earaches at nighttime. I had hot temperatures and ringing in my ears.

Inside my ear was wet and
I couldn't hear very well. I was
often sad because of the pain.

Then, the Earbus visited my school, and the nurse and doctor checked my ears.

They washed my sore ear and gave me ear drops.

They gave me medicine and soon I felt better!

The Earbus team taught me how to look after my ears.

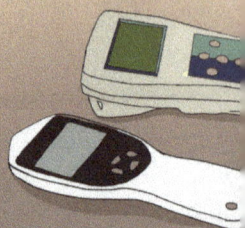

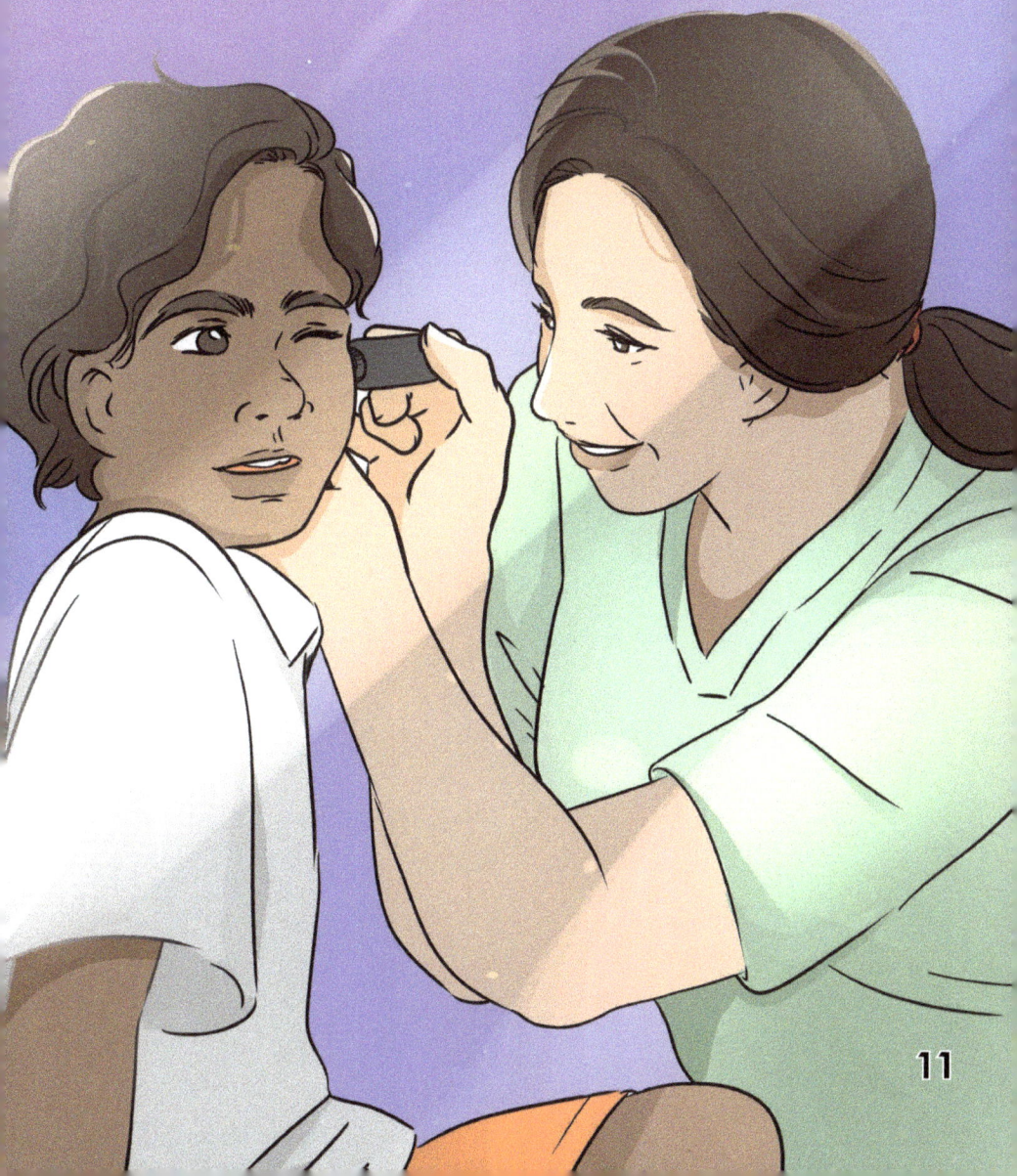

I went back to the Earbus for checkups and a hearing test.

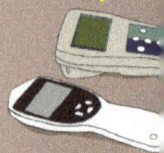

Beep! Beep! went the ear pressure machine.

The light shining into my ear showed a hole in my eardrum.

The Earbus doctor sent me to
see a specialist ear doctor
at the clinic.

The ear specialist said I must wait until I am bigger for more treatment.

She showed me how to keep my ears dry, so they didn't ache.

She told me to keep my ear dry with tissue spears.

I was not allowed to put my head under the water when I was swimming.

Now, I'm bigger and my ear is fixed. *YAY!*

I can hear my pop's stories, the teachers at school and, best of all, go to the beach and surf when it's hot.

Look after your ears with the
BBCEWC program!

I blow my nose.
I check if it's empty.
I take 5 deep breaths.
I do 2 strong coughs into my elbow.
I do 10 star jumps to warm up.
I do my 5 breaths and 2 coughs again.
I run on the spot for a little bit.
I do my breaths and coughs again
and...

WHEW!

I wash my hands really well.

Then I eat a crunchy snack!

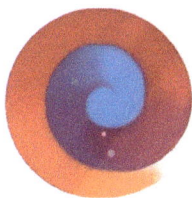

earbus
foundation of WA

BBCEWC PROGRAM

THE BLOW, BREATHE, COUGH, EXERCISE, WASH AND CHEW PROGRAM

1. **BLOW YOUR NOSE**

2. **BREATHS IN THROUGH THE NOSE & OUT THROUGH THE MOUTH**

3. **COUGH INTO THE ELBOW**

4. **EXERCISE EVERYDAY**

5. **WASH YOUR HANDS**

6. **CRUNCH & MUNCH TIME**

You can use these questions to talk about this book with your family, friends and teachers.

What did you learn from this book?

Describe this book in one word. Funny? Scary? Colourful? Interesting?

How did this book make you feel when you finished reading it?

What was your favourite part of this book?

About the author

Chance and his family are from the Noongar Nation and live in Eaton, Western Australia. He likes playing sports, making art, and being with his family.

Author's Country

Our Yarning

The Our Yarning collection aligns with the Australian Curriculum through the Cross-Curriculum Priorities — Aboriginal and Torres Strait Islander Histories and Cultures. The collection provides an authentic opportunity for learning and embedding Aboriginal and Torres Strait Islander perspectives because it is written by Aboriginal and Torres Strait Islander people.

We know that children learn better, and enjoy reading more, when they see themselves in the stories, characters and illustrations of the books they read.

To download the app, visit the Google Play Store or Apple Store and search 'Our Yarning'.

libraryforall.org

You're reading Level 3

Learner – Beginner readers

Start your reading journey with short words, big ideas and plenty of pictures.

Level 1 – Rising readers

Raise your reading level with more words, simple sentences and exciting images.

Level 2 – Eager readers

Enjoy your reading time with familiar words, but complex sentences.

Level 3 – Progressing readers

Develop your reading skills with creative stories and some challenging vocabulary.

Level 4 – Fluent readers

Step up your reading skills with playful narratives, new words and fun facts.

Middle Primary – Curious readers

Discover your world through science and stories.

Upper Primary – Adventurous readers

Explore your world through science and stories.

Library For All is an Australian not for profit organisation with a mission to make knowledge accessible to all via an innovative digital library solution. Visit us at libraryforall.org

Ears That Hear

First published 2024

Published by Library For All Ltd
Email: info@libraryforall.org
URL: libraryforall.org

Original BBCEWC poster on page 23 created by Sammi Fatnowna, and shared with permission. For further information, contact sammi.fatnowna@gmail.com.

Library For All would like to thank Chance Little's school for their support in this project. Djidi Aboriginal School, Glen Iris, Western Australia.

Our Yarning logo design by Jason Lee, Bidjipidji Art

Original illustrations by Keishart

Ears That Hear
Little, Chance
ISBN: 978-1-923207-05-9
SKU04319

www.ingramcontent.com/pod-product-compliance
Lightning Source LLC
Chambersburg PA
CBHW042342040426
42448CB00019B/3371